a woman in pieces

Nicole Cannon

Bainbridge Island Press

a woman

in pieces
Nicole Cannon

Bainbridge Island Press
Bainbridge Island, WA

A Woman in Pieces by Nicole Cannon
Copyright © 2025
All rights reserved

Published in 2025 by Bainbridge Island Press
Bainbridge Island, WA
https://bainbridgeisland.press

Printed in the United States of America

ISBN: 978-1-961451-10-0
Library of Congress Control Number: 2025934705

Cover & Book Design: Ben Rockwood
Editor: Tamarah Rockwood

9 8 7 6 5 4 3 2 1

for the feminine in all of us

Acknowledgments

The author acknowledges the editors of the following publications in which some of these poems in this book previously appeared:

Words & Whispers Issue 12:
    "Unknown Void"

Side-Eye on the Apocalypse Anthology:
    "Earthly Cravings"

ONTHEBUS 23- Not the Last Issue:
    "redwood"
    "The Whole Way Down"
    "Attaining Enlightenment in the Wild Wild West"

Method Writers Speak Number 4
    "Autumnal Eclipses: Closing Out Karmic Contracts"

Many thanks to Jack Grapes for helping me find my voice. My deepest gratitude to my children, Celeste and Remi Cannon, and my mother/sister/friend Michelle Burack for inspiring me every day to fully embrace and integrate the wholeness of womanhood.

Contents

CHILD

Carnival	3
Cleopatra's Tears	4
the recipe of me	5
reborn	6
The Places She Goes	7
MIA	9
The Movie of Life	10
ensnared	11
Tune Up	12
learning about racism [i didn't know]	13

VIRGIN

Wrought Iron	19
Something Borrowed	20
Spackle	21
S O N G	22
unanswered	24
The Stone	25
egg separator	26
Petals of a Dazey Fall	28
In Japan I started dreaming again	30
errands	32
( )	33

MOTHER

Purple Heart	35
The Proposal	36
Unmothered	38
Lightning	39
Dark Matter	40
flesh and blood	41

bones and feathers   42
Caul Bearer   44
The Whole Way Down   45
Pulling Taffy   46
Untethering   48

SIREN

Lotus Flower   51
The Lovers   52
Ebb and Flow   53
Drawing from Reference   54
surrender   55
Loveletting   56
Uncalloused   57
The Feast   58
unveiling   59
When Death Comes Calling   60

MEDUSA

New Moon   63
Indispensable   64
The American Dream / Mass Destruction   66
Sunday Mornings   67
Life Expectancy of a Telescope Mirror   68
The Wall   69
child restraints   70
Woman in Pieces   72
Snake Skin   76
DIY Stroke   78
The Gap   79
Autumnal Eclipses: closing out karmic contracts   80
The Salesman   82

HUNTRESS

The Last Soliloquy	85
Unknown Void	86
hide n' seek	89
quiet	90
The call is coming from inside the house.	92
me vs me	94
Perfectionism	95
i didn't write a poem today	96
Sutra of Karma	98
Attaining Enlightenment in the Wild Wild West	99
you will be met	100

CRONE

Release	103
Darn	104
De-struction	106
Grief	108
Primal Urges	110
letting go	111
Night Mer	114
redwood	115
Welcoming the Witch	116
Earthly Cravings	118
If a tree screams in the forest and no one hears, did it fall?	120

About the author	123

a woman in pieces

Nicole Cannon

CHILD

Carnival

I was in bumper cars apologizing until I looked above the electrified cage and saw each car had its own blob of clay-like matter directing it where to go and I realized, "This is what we're meant to do down here. Bump into each other."

Cleopatra's Tears

This being. A filter of energy
expressed as Nicole-ness
with all of its karmic
ties
and
bondage

This body. It's cellular stories
replaying inter-gene-rational
DNA all the way
back
back
back
through the evolution of humanity

Once upon a time
we were single-celled
squirming through
primordial ooze
fighting for survival—
still energy.

The construct of my mind
the meaning I give
my existence
keeping me attached and "secure"—
a Ni-coal-ness pressed into diamond.

But then they say diamonds rain on Saturn and Jupiter

the recipe of me

accumulated energies

of

experience and identities

impacts

then leaves

indents

in the ether

a portal of re-entry

for my entity

reborn

in the winter
she loves to run away
from her mother
barefoot in her pajamas
out to the fresh laid snow

in the spring
she loves to feel
the crumbling ice crunch
beneath her feet
water droplets fall
from icicles
keeping time
as they melt
sparkling in the sun

in the summer
she makes mud pies
and feeds her friends—
the aspen trees
she paints their trunks
with her faerie concoction
of wildflower, moss and placental earth

in the fall
she wanders from home
when the sun is low and golden
to lay down in the forest decay
and listen to the wind chime
through the aspen cathedral

[she is born again]

The Places She Goes

In a fit of grief
she thought,
'If I wasn't me, who would I be?'

It opened a portal to
an
  other
no
  thing
and gave her
a funny feeling

The kind of funny
you feel when a word
repeated too many times
loses its meaning
like
promise
promise
promise
promise

When she was four
her older sister asked,
"What do you want
to be
when you grow up?"

She didn't yet know
what an
I
even was
to be
much less wanting
to be an
I

Her sister persisted,
"You can be
any
  thing
you want
to be."

On the desk

was a giant picture book
with a brontosaurus
on the cover
swampy greens dripping
from its mouth,
pterodactyls swooping
in the distant sky.

"When I grow up,"
she said,
"I want to be a dinosaur."

MIA

Since she landed
at Miami International
I haven't been very lucky

I got lost
over the Bermuda triangle

I've been loose
change and in-counters
with strange change

been rolled up an' banked
behind bars
from state to state
I've broken bills
but never charged

It's been all
take one, leave one
at the five an' dime
wishin' wells
gumball machines
I've done some time

One kid found me
in the gutter
an' polished me off

I was just passin' through
his digestive tract
an' got flushed down
washed up
metal detected an' collected

in thrift stores, estate sales
a vintage Chanel coat

After twenty long years
she reaches in the pocket
an' pulls out a ball of lint
an old stick of Wrigley's
an' me, her lucky
Liberty Lady penny

The Movie of Life

We see through
the I
the lens

the eye
the aperture

filter in
block out

Light
Dark

blink and shudder

the flutter
the film

The stage
the Earth

The players
project!

Choose to view
a story of Love
not violence

After all it's
starring
        Space
&
co-starring
        Time
ever after.

ensnared

i am a dinosaur
pressed into
crude oil
sucked
up a pump-jack
and turned into plastic wrap
disposed of
i escaped from a dumpster
tumbled and worn down to
wispy shreds
i drifted
grifted the 101
and snagged
on the branch
of a weed
pushing up
through cracks of the asphalt
as traffic breezed by

when i am set free
i will float into
the upper atmosphere
where i am broken by the sun
dissolved
down
into molecules
of carbon hydrogen and chloride
to be reassembled
into something new

Tune Up

This morning I could hear my synapses firing
like high frequency radio waves. I opened a drawer
in my head. There was my brain. A super computer
cycling through the same program repetitively.

I considered tampering but it was much
too complex for me. When the technician arrived
she asked what was wrong with it. I said, "Nothing!
It runs perfect. I would just like it to run a bit more quietly."

learning about racism [i didn't know]

in kindergarten
my best friend
was Tabitha Greene

we learned together
played together
ate together

in the classroom
recess and lunch

i loved her
long curly
eyelashes

her beautiful
brown skin

her style

the gentleness
in her eyes

how her spirit
carried
her petit frame
with so much grace and dignity

her hair
everyday a different style
with colored
ties, clips and bows

Tabby's mom
was a 1st grade teacher
i hoped
we would be
in the same class

the next year
i came back
excited to see my friend

she wouldn't
look at me

in the hallways
talk
at recess
play
in the yard
have lunch

i didn't know
what happened

maybe she forgot
about me
over the summer
i didn't know

maybe
i repeated
something
my father
said
he was racist
i didn't know

or maybe because
i always liked
to play with her hair
i didn't know

in fifth grade
i told
my grandmother
visiting
from out of state
i was afraid
to go to school
because
two black girls
didn't like me
she
used the n-word
and called the school

i loved
Miss Culver
the librarian

she read to us

showed us filmstrips
found us books
ran the projector
even when
it jammed
and the reel broke
in sixth grade
she found a crumpled-up note
on one of the book shelves
while my class
was at library

they made
the class
write "n-word like Miss Culver"
on a piece of paper
and turn it in

Miss Culver was crying
as they compared
each of them
side by side

i didn't know
how to spell the n-word
and maybe
that was the point
of the test
i'll never know

they didn't
directly
accused
any of us

when we got back to class
our teacher Mrs. Gendron
said
in her
thick Southern accent

"i'm sure whoever wrote
that note
meant no harm
they coulda
just been sayin
my friend is a

nnnnnn-wooooord
like Miss Culver"
when i was sixteen
i was captain of a
competition cheerleading squad
i named our team
scrolling through the list of
emblems and mascots
trying on them all
one by one

Palm Bay Chiefs
Palm Bay Indians
Palm Bay Pirates
Palm Bay Rebels

i liked the sound of it
going against the grain
girls in it for themselves
cheering for our own wins
a rebellion
against my father

we held up
handmade signs
with the confederate flags
in our bikinis
for $5 car washes at
at local gas station

we knocked
door to door
in the neighborhood
wearing uniforms
asking for donations
to get us to Nationals

one of my girls said
a man refused
to donate
and *we* were the ones
offended
when he told her
before closing the door
"rebels are very bad people"

it did not even occur

to me
until years
too many years
after i left Florida
why

it's taken years
too many years
for me
to unlearn
racism

i am still…unlearning

VIRGIN

Wrought Iron

Our children are born in sterile hospitals. Hazmat containers carry away the remnants of love. We've been taught to wrap our life force, stop up and flush down Earth's vitality, while She drinks our hatred and fear on the battlefield.

Something Borrowed

She was gawky
with self-conscious adolescence.

Not at all sweet
with her nipple buds
poking through her t-shirt.

Pretty, but much too old
to be a flower girl.

Her mother made friends
with the owner
of Petty's Meat Market.

So something borrowed
became scattered petals
down the aisle
at the butcher's wedding.

And from that day on
chuck roast was only
three bucks a pound.

Spackle

She nestles
into people,

likes to be the putty
that fills
their cracks,

or the glue that holds
their psyche.

The last time she felt
held this tight,

was as an embryo
implanted
within uterine walls.

SONG

There was a girl

whose heart
was a bank vault
made of words

coarse and abrasive

locked in
solitary
for years

forever lost…

in the silence
between things
until an explosion

alpha-bets in bits

swept into heaps
and ground down
to sound

A U M

vibration
pushed against
the darkness

NOTHINGNESS

Words are reeds
that feelings
flow through

...lost then found

they fall short
in resonance
made meaning

LOVE

a vibration
rippling towards
the light

EVERYTHING

in existence
is
a song

unanswered

the question
hangs in the air
after two people part

the karmic ghost
left in their passing

that vacuums
them back together

lifetime
after
lifetime
after
lifetime
like the infinity mirror

lovers echo
in each other
only to break apart
once more

The Stone

Arguments are like peaches.
If you pick them when they're ripe
you can pull them apart
in equal halves
and take out the stone.
Then both can enjoy
the nectar.

If plucked too soon
no matter how you slice it
sour flesh
always sticks
to the pit.

egg separator

I was last minute shopping
the Christmas after my divorce
listening to the young couple
in the checkout line
talking about eggs.

I could tell it was a new relationship.

He was carrying their basket of presents
hair slicked, shirt tucked, pants belted
nervous and earnest
talking about eggs.

She was all dressed up
in eyelash extensions, lip gloss, heels
insecure and attentive
listening to him
talking about eggs.

"I want to get an egg separator," he stammered,
 "Because, well, I'm being smart and eating egg whites now."

In a flash I see
his life of egg white omelets
and the sweaty gym
where he battles cholesterol
to woo her
with his lean muscle mass.

"Oh," she says,
hinting she knows her way
around the kitchen,
"you can use the shells to do that too."

I see their future
with kids and bills
the last minute purchases
and no more talks about eggs.
She'll just take the unnecessary
items out of their basket
put them back without a word.

But in this moment
he's sincere
and she's devout.

And I think, maybe
this is what love is about
just hanging out
talking about eggs.

Petals of a Dazey Fall

He held my gaze
at coffee
He loves me

He did the same with the barista
I guess it's his "thing"
He loves me not

He texted and asked
when
we could
meet again
He loves me

He canceled
our plans to meet
at the dog park
last minute
He loves me not

He liked
my selfie
He loves me

He liked 3 other
sexy girls' selfies too
He loves me not

ding ding
text message
HE LOVES ME

It's not him
He loves me not

He picked me up
on a Saturday night
and took me to Blossom
An actual real date
We totally hit it off
He definitely loves me

He said
he'd call
the next day
It's been three weeks
I love him not

In Japan I started dreaming again

some dreams
feel real

still
with me
from the boundless
place

like when
he held
my face
and said, "i've been
waiting for you,"

his large hand
wrapped around
my neck and face
grounding me
in non-physical

impressions

expressions

"you're here.
you're real.
the girl
in my dreams.
i will find you.
i will find you.
we are already
in each other.
i will find you…"

i believed him

the way he
held me in
the subconscious
realm

i was real
for him too

he told
me his name
before i awoke

it means
a protective
guiding force

i guess
this is hope

errands

He said he's afraid of love
so I promised myself
not to scare him away.

I don't say the words
but do it anyway.

He's also afraid
of spiders —
I keep one in the car,
a jumping wolf spider
named Fred.

The other day
when we were
running errands
he thought it
dropped into his hair.

I smiled
while he shouted
and stomped
and swatted
it away.

He doesn't know yet,

I am the one in his hair.

(   )

this space
i hold
for you
remains

nameless

for once
it's brought
into form
it risks the fate
of gravity and time

can a love
that is named
be borne
without breaking

i sift through
warm ash

MOTHER

Purple Heart

Everyone you meet has chosen this life and should be honored as warriors. Embattled in the struggle of separation and longing. Traversing the constructs of love and identity. Hunkered down in human suffering, I wave a white flag.

The Proposal

When I lived on the Venetian Islands
I had a Weimaraner puppy
a little blue girl named Skye.

Across the street
behind an electric gate
lived an older silver male.

When I took Skye for a walk
we'd stop by the gentledog's
house for a sniff, to say hello.

This excited the lonely canine.
He would stand tall
his docked tale erect and wagging.

On one occasion
he lifted a leg and released
his scented mark
to claim her as his own.

I immediately yanked
her away from the stream
and we stopped paying our daily visits.

Every day I'd see him waiting
for Skye at the gate
hoping to catch her eye.

He'd pace back and forth in his yard
worried he'd blown
his only shot at love.

Early one morning
Old Grey bolted across the street
carrying something in his mouth
and dropped it at Skye's feet.

He took a step back and stood tall
pleased with himself
tail erect and wagging.

He waited for her response
She didn't know what to do.
She had never seen, smelled, much less tasted
an entire roasted chicken carcass in her life.

She couldn't know
the amount of planning,
patience and restraint
it took for Old Grey to steal
the remains from the trash, hide
it in a safe place until morning, time
his owner leaving for work, retrieve
the precious jewel, slip
through the closing gate, wait
undetected for his beloved in the street, restrain
the urge to indulge himself
so he could make this
offering of love and devotion.

Skye looked up at me
with the most innocent gaze.
I have to admit I was quite charmed
by Old Grey's gesture.

Even still, I scooped her up safely in my arms
"Don't worry sweetheart," I said
"I'm not going to give you to him."

Unmothered

I could have so much
love for a woman
who left me in the mountains
by a barbed wire fence post
to fend for herself.

She knew
the way only a mother knows
how much her child
is like herself, best left
in the wild, raised
by the wolves.

She was only twenty.
At nineteen I left mine
in a biohazard waste container
at the clinic, high on nitrous
unwilling to make her
mistake.

I won a beauty pageant
five weeks pregnant
with my dealer's baby.
His mother paid
for the entry fee,
the airfare and the procedure.
My ticket out
of her fate.

Unmothered girls who turn
into unmothered women become
unmothered mothers
unmothered murderers
of unmothered children.

This poem feels incomplete.
Maybe that's how it should be—
a child unmet,
a life unlived.
Think of it as compassion
for the unborn.

Lightning

All of their firsts. Every
giggle. Every heartbreak
and scraped knee. Each new
discovery. All the lopsided
art. Whispers at bedtime. Sticky
fingers on the walls. The screams
for independence. Nuzzles
of forgiveness. Pride. The pain
of letting go. Their return.
She wanted it all back.
And like a bolt, it came.
Sixteen years in one second.

Dark Matter

I found my Mother in emptiness
and She filled the space
between things.

She is in immeasurable things
like love and nurturance and kindness.
She is invisible. The unseen thing.
Weaving her way through all of the cells
and molecules and atoms.

She is in everything. The glue that binds
the moons to their planets and the planets
to their stars and the stars to their solar systems
and the solar systems to their galaxies.

She is Dark Matter, the soil.
She and Energy have a Love child
and its name is *Life*.

flesh and blood

I can still feel you
my flesh.
The moment they took you from me
your smell
new. metallic. pure.
and placed you on my loose skin
Discovery.

Not yet
separate
entity.
Mewl
Discovery.
You are not me
but we are one.
Our snuggles
calibration.

bones and feathers

It was selfish having children,
my desire to be whole.
Psychologically, I eat my young
to make up for lost innocence.

My 17-year-old swears
she doesn't want kids. Her boyfriend
gave her a rare breed chicken egg
for her birthday.

I heard them on the phone
after it hatched,
worrying about the new chick
if it had pooped yet.

She's hatching quail eggs too.
The first one pipped
its tiny beak
through the thick dry shell
and died before
it made its way
into the world.

We watched over
the others for the next four days.
The eggs wobbled and rocked
in their struggle towards life.

I wanted to help them out.
"No!" said Celeste,
"They're not ready, you'll kill them."

She is the child of nature, bird whisperer,
gatherer of bones and feathers—
capture, study and release,
conserver of her "main girl" Earth.

"The struggle makes them stronger,"
she whispers, holding me back
with mother-like wisdom.

Her teachers emailed
that she's been missing assignments.
I didn't tell them
it's because of the new babies,
but scolded Celeste for her falling grades.

The charge in my words
is my father's disappointment
in me—my head always in the clouds.
Celeste's is with the birds.

When she was in kindergarten
she asked why we weren't born
knowing everything,
so we didn't have to go to school.
I pushed her out the door.

Soon, she'll leave the nest;
I worry she's not ready.
Still, I push from my womb
into the world.

Caul Bearer

I was already four centimeters dilated
before I went into labor
with my second daughter.
In the weeks leading up
to her birth, I'd feel
an occasional pinch at my cervix,
like she was eating her way out.

I'd shout, "Ouch!"
lift my belly and drop it in response,
adjusting the fetus to find comfort again—
our first fight about freedom.

I imagine her
in the pitch-black darkness,
searching around for a weak spot
that would give way to her prodding—
a portal into a larger world
where she could be more of herself.

Once out, she had a favorite blanket named Foofy.
It wasn't just the blanket she loved,
but a loose Loop of yarn near the corner.
At bedtime she'd lie in her crib,
fix her eyes on the border,
and hand over hand search for her Loop.
"I'm wooking fo' my woop," she'd murmur,
and slide her pinky finger through the opening.
Finally secure she'd found her portal,
she'd drift off to her dream world.

One morning she woke—
her pinky bloated and purple,
strangled by the blanket twisted in the night.
I snipped the thread and broke that sutra
through which she finds comfort and liberation.
Blood rushed to the heart
gasping for oxygen—
like that first solo breath
when the cord was cut,
and she was free of me.

The Whole Way Down

I took my girls to a water park when they were little.
My oldest wanted to go on a big girl slide called The Black Hole.
It was a giant enclosed black tube that spiraled down forever.

My youngest is terrified of the dark.
She took one look at the water rushing
into the gaping mouth of the black abyss
and refused to get in the raft.

I promised I would hold onto her
the whole way down.

The three of us got in and huddled
to one side of the raft.
We screamed and laughed
sloshed and spun and wobbled
in the pitch black *down down down*
the spiral slide until we burst through
to the bright white light of the day
and plunged with a splash
into the lucid pool below.

I have this image of Americans
in the Mid-West wearing hazmat suits
sweeping up ash and soot from nuclear fallout
while the tangerine man broadcasts
from his underground bunker bragging
how unemployment and overpopulation
are at an all-time low.

I read it would take 33 minutes or less
for an enemy ballistic missile to reach us.
I hope it's my week with the kids if the bomb goes off.

I hope we're just about to sit down for dinner
when every Smart Phone in the world
sounds an alarm in unison
warning us to take cover.

"No phones at the dinner table," I'll remind them.
"Turn them off."

And we hold onto each other the whole way *down*.

Pulling Taffy

As young children
we are often
presented with the most difficult
of existential questions
before we are fully formed.

What do you want to *Be*
when you grow up?

The onus of becoming
replaces the wonder of being.

We look to the outside
to define us
and become decorator crabs
of our experience
carrying each event
on our back
hardening us against life.

A mother sees her child
carry this burden
and wants to lighten the load.

Herein lies the Tug.
The simultaneous push and pull
between mother and daughter.

Motherhood is a constant
weighing of when to step in
and rescue
and when to back off
so the child may find
their own equilibrium.

The child feels the Tug too.
The yearning for discovery
amalgamated with a longing
for the safety of home.

Life has not given you
your experiences
to carry as you go
out into the world.
You already
have everything
you need inside of you.

The Tug is there
to stretch you
like pulling taffy
so you don't harden
against the sweetness of life.

Untethering

For my 40th birthday
I took a pilgrimage to Mount Kailash,
the abode of Shiva, the final
resting place of Buddha
where the Jains, Rishabhanatha
attained Nirvana.

It was there
in a guided meditation,
my kundalini rising, I merged
into the boundlessness I always longed for.

With my breath all aflutter at sixteen thousand feet,
moans of Ecstasy bursting
from my lips in a full blown Shivagasm,
I felt I could step out of my body,
but for two points of attachment:

woman and mother

If only I could cut
those two cords
I would be free
but I promised not
to leave my children
like she did.

My eldest daughter
leaves for college in September.
Pride and loss mix in me like oil and water.

I left home at eighteen and never
looked back.
How can I re-mother myself
when she's so far away?

I am at fifty straddling the chasm
of identity lost
at a crossroads, stuck
in limbo, frozen
smack dab in the middle
of duality—waiting
for the metronome to swing
and knock me into the ravine.

I have been going for long
hikes in the wilderness of Ojai
past the crepuscular hour,
tempting death to choose me.

I might be using fear
as a defibrillator to jolt
me back into life,
help find a way
into the next chapter.

I took a solo-journey
on a mushroom spaceship,
ego shedding and seeking answers.

I found myself trapped in bed
for a good part of the evening crying,
tangled in wet linen,
writhing in the pain
of having to let go of my babies,
grieving the loss 'til mourning
all of them—
my Earth babies too.

The thread of motherhood
cannot be cut.
It is what the whole
of existence is woven from,
yet I still
long to be free.

SIREN

Lotus Flower

Sitting lotus inside AUM, beyond the limitations of human love, outside the concepts and constructs I've used to protect and define a self; the vibration of the union and separation of the energetic masculine/feminine principles ebb and flow. That magnetic field, both creative and destructive, emanates constant pure unconditional LOVE. Creation.

The Lovers

Before I found him
I didn't believe
our kind of love existed
on the Earth plane

But then again
how could my soul
find anyone
without a body

It is only through
Earth's vibration
that our bodily senses
can truly feel
what we are

Love

Union

God

Soulmates
energy matches
ignites and burns
transmutes or fades

From form
into nothingness
and back again
for eternity

Ebb and Flow

He wraps me up in a tiny ball
and pulls me into him
again...
        again...
                again...

and I dissolve
into the crest of a wave
that never breaks on shore
but tumbles
further...
        further...
                further...

out to sea
roiling
up and over and under
again...
        again...
                again...

churning
the deepest waters
of my blue ocean

Drawing from Reference

I retrace
the contour
of the living sculpture
lying beside me,

grazing
with my eyes
the territory
my mouth
just claimed,

mapping
the light
that rests
along
the landscape
of his body,

the fine line
that defines
the space
between
emptiness
and
everything
that exists.

surrender

surges that swell
in the dark
bring me to my edge
and crash along the shore

then

peace

until

the echo ripples
back across the misty stillness
at dawn

leaving me helpless
but to ride out these
undulations

Loveletting

If what Rumi
and Leonard
say is true
the sun should be
where my heart
once was.

Hot, molten
liquid love
solar flares
radiating from
my chest
interfering with
the radio signals
from my brain.

Every time
I choose
to love
it burns.

Uncalloused

For years
when the man,
who couldn't
receive
my love,
opened his mouth—
I shuddered.

Words
between us,
coarse and abrasive,
wore down all
my sharp edges,
until I lost myself
in silence.

Now this mouth
makes
my lover
tremble.

It's no wonder
my lips
want to graze
every part of him.

They're the only thing
left of me
uncalloused.

Pressed against
the edge of him
and at once
I am found.

The Feast

We were both lost
not lost but
searching our paths
for the path home.
The way
he looked into me
when I told him
I was forging
my own desire trails
stopped my foraging,
this incessant search
for breadcrumbs.

unveiling

reveal

as we continue
to unfold

opportunity comes
with each new layer

to find each other
again

reveil

When Death Comes Calling

Death visits me
in my meditation.

He gives me a single red poppy.

Death is coy,
hiding behind his tattered robes and scythe.

I can't decipher
if the flower is an apology or flirtation,
so I research the symbol.

In the West, red poppies
are linked to remembrance and consolation.
Maybe he is offering me condolences
for taking my sweet puppy too soon.

In the East, red poppies
mean a deep and passionate love
between couples.

I don't know how
I'm going to introduce
my new boyfriend
to my parents.

MEDUSA

New Moon

Once wild and cycling with the moon, hematic tides lured vicious hunger. Iron willed and scented she led away doom. Selflessness drove them asunder. Howling at night in the cold with no Moon, fear replaced love left lone in his gloom.

Indispensable

At twenty, I had my
first existential crisis
not knowing
the purpose of me.

I called my father sobbing
"Why am I here?"
The static of silence
between us.

"Are you on drugs?"
his voice trembling,
he was scared—
I could tell.

He was worried
I would end up
a "fuck-up"
like my mother
at twenty.

"You're here," he said,
"because you make me happy."

I want to empathize with him
not knowing what to tell
his child suffering
two thousand miles away
but I didn't call
to comfort him.

Even as a kid
crushed by existence,
I didn't call
across the hall
to him for comfort.

Instead, I would imagine
my death—not by my own hand,
but death by negligence,
death by accident,

getting hit
by a car,

drowning
in the ocean,

or, if I was feeling romantic
falling into a volcano.

Over the next
twenty-five years
my purpose
translated
from making my father happy
to making a man happy.

I've changed
my friends
my clothes
my music
my dreams
my identity

to make a man happy

I've learned
to cook
to fuck
to empathize
to take the blame
to look the other way

to make a man happy

I've bargained
my youth
my money
my body
my dignity
my self

to make a man happy

All in the name of love
at least, that's what they thought.
What I was really doing
was making myself
indispensable.

The American Dream / Mass Destruction

The white pickets
were the bars of my prison
There wasn't enough love
in our marriage
to fill eighty-five hundred square feet

He said he bought it for me
but I wasn't up
for the role of perfect wife

What he bought
was the American dream
he grew up on, *watchin'*
'is programs on the telly
eatin' boil in a bag
with his mum passed out
drunk since noon
on the settee

When I moved out
I left an old Nike shoebox
full of dildos
on the top shelf of the walk-in closet
the size of a New York apartment

The Rabbit, the blown glass,
the silicone porn star replica
popping veins and all—
5-speeds, 10-settings
waterproof, rechargeable
remote-controlled, manual
semi-automatic
weapons
of
mass
destruction
He said he bought them for me

Then I caught him using Viagra
that he didn't buy for me

Sunday Mornings

the secure crook
of your arm
my pillow

morning light
covers
linen like dew

our slow talks
open doors
in my heart

your gentle hand
guides me down
the spiral staircase

to the bottom step
where I tremble
without walls

you find what
you need

and gather pyramidal stacks
of my vulnerabilities
into your arsenal

Life Expectancy of a Telescope Mirror

The life expectancy
of a telescope mirror is
10-20 years

depending on the
conditions
in which it's kept.

His was the reflection
of epic loneliness
whose only cure was pity
til death do us part.

I faced mine alone
and brought it
Light, Compassion
and Forgiveness.

The life expectancy
of a telescope mirror is
10-20 years

unless you're the one to break it.

Then it's seven years
bad luck.

I'll take
my chances.

The Wall

Here's what I know about walls
and the people who build them:
they are built tall,
but have no reach;
they are built from the inside out,
new bricks laid
not from top to bottom,
but bottom to top.

The architect stands on high
looking down on all others.
He builds with fear and denigration,
to convince contractors
to carry out his construction.

Its promise is greatness,
but its only purpose is to raise him up.

Step inside
and you'll see the truth.
He forges bricks
from skulls,
from hearts,
from hopes.

He stomps on each one
as he claws his way
to the top.

Chained to the ground,
at the base of the wall—
his wounded inner child.

All he wants is love,
and if you give it to him,
he will chop off your head
with his trowel.

child restraints

it was past our bedtime
after the electric light parade
and the Magic Kingdom
grand finale

sensory overload
on the ferry ride
back to the parking lot
from a full day
of surreal
everything

Pluto C365

four adults
and four children
piled into the blue Ford
station wagon

there were no
child restraint
laws
back then

my sister and i
crammed in the cargo area
sleeping
with the strollers
pressed against my back

one toddler
riding shotgun
on my stepmother's lap

the other wedged
between my
father's work friend and
his lovely pregnant wife

from the rearview mirror
it may have looked
to my father
that his work friend's
outstretched arm
along the seat

was wrapped around
his lovely pregnant wife

on
that
long
hour
ride
home

and he might
have heard me,
fighting with my sister
for more room
as she pushed
away from
the seat back,

if we didn't feel
the need
to whisper
when his work friend
kept trying
to reach inside
my sister's panties

we were trained early
to keep quiet
while men do
their searching
in the dark

to this day
i wonder,
if my sister had sat up
and screamed
"Stop it you creep!"
my dad would have
pulled the car over
and left him bloody
on the side of the road

Woman in Pieces

Boardwalk
Eden Roc
October of '95

I'm a model running
through blades and cycles
I sense
the untold story
hidden in plain sight

the downtrodden
boy
in his twenties delayed
shuffles behind
an angry stride
violent eyed
rageful pride
Father
the only thing
missing was his
leash and collar

Dolce and Gabbana
Beverly Center
November of '98

I was a sales girl
on the floor pushing
stretch denim flying
off the racks.

Black Friday,
in walks in
Madame
and a young Korean girl.

I size her up
she's pale
much too pale
"May I help you?"
eyes concealed
puffy purple
cast down to the ground.

She's thin
much too thin
hips tucked under
in abject concession
like a shamed dog
that's made a piddle
on the floor
"These are our best sellers" I say.
"24 inch waste."

They share a Korean exchange
helpless compliance
"*Please*, let me help you" I whisper
but a deal is sealed
silence is bought
for a $220 pair of jeans
made in a sweatshop
for less than she is paid
for the night.

Public Bathroom
West Hollywood Park
December of '99

I was a teacher's helper
at a preschool
on a field trip

a little girl
had to go
I was asked to take her
checking the stall
to make sure it was
clean and safe
laying down
the tissue cover
and lifting her
onto the seat

I told her "I'll stay
if you want me to"
forgetting
big girls
don't need help

going potty

her brown eyes
looked up at me
trust turned to fear
worried
I might feed
my lost innocence
by stealing hers

my babysitter did
when I was three
trusting him
to find the missing tag
from my panties
lost in my vagina

Ralph's Market
Brentwood
January 2010

I am a mother
caught in a storm
an old woman
blind from syphilis
missed her bus
her bulk paper goods
melt in the rain
I call her a taxi
she doesn't speak english
so the address I give is wrong
to an abandoned warehouse
on the south side
instead the cabbie drops her
jane doe
at the nearest precinct

Pashupatinath Temple
Kathmandu
August 2011

I am a pilgrim
trekking the Himalayas
two Nepalese sisters
follow us

Sightseeing, I buy
a handwoven purse and glass beads
My twinkle of gratitude
is mistaken for lust—
a much bigger payout
then selling
trifles and trinkets
on the streets
for a meal

Bowing down to Shiva
through Nepal and Tibet
I pray they know
the love
in my eyes
was not
solicitation
but communion

This survivor
recognizes
those survivors.

Snake Skin

I slid out of my teenage angst
a snake shedding
its skin the night I decided
to leave my marriage.

If I had seen in my father's disapproving eyes
the child in him cowering
in the closet of his childhood bedroom
hoping the belt wouldn't find him again
would I have turned out different?

His words were my belt
every six weeks since I was thirteen
he worried aloud to my tear-soaked,
puffy-eyed, snot-nosed face
I would end like my mother—
a fuck up— for not coming home
with good grades.

When my father looked at me
he saw her—his heartbreak,
his loss, his failure.

I left home at eighteen.
My mother's demons called me
to come find her. His ghosts followed
into the bathrooms of night clubs
where strangers offered things
to snort, lick, swallow and huff.
I could never escape
his disappointed eyes
in my hallucinations.

I dropped deeper until I found my lost mother
and looked into that mercurial mirror.
I was nothing like her.
I could never leave my children.

When my girls were eight and six
I told my husband I wanted a divorce.
"Just go," he said, "We'll be fine without you."
It took me four years to reply, "I'm not
leaving them, I'm leaving you."
This time my father's ghost did not follow.

My oldest daughter turns
eighteen next week. She'll leave soon.
Her angels come to calm my fears
so that my worried thoughts
won't find her.

DIY Stroke

She went into debt
trying to get her girls back
though we were right there in front of her

She looked at me with muddy goggles
of guilt and shame
I must have looked like a swamp thing
pleading my love to her

She worked a 60-hour week
to keep from sinking
waiting on fancy customers
always with the bog
beneath her nail beds.

She went bankrupt at Home Depot
buying flats of flowers
to make a beautiful home
so she could get her girls back

Though we'd already grown
with homes and kids of our own.

Now she sleeps in her own sick
Sometimes she eats it
to hide it from the nurse
who only works the late shift
so she won't have to change
diapers and shovel shit.

They'll send her to a home soon
that smells of piss and bleach
where she'll never get us back.

The Gap

I've been nursing a shame hangover all month.

I'd fuck it away
but that's what got me
into this mess
in the first place.

I had a nice romance
with a sweet boy once
but my art suffered for it.

I like messy and complicated.

My brain needs
a mystery
I can't solve.

My heart longs
to be the glue that holds
them together.

My body desires
to be crushed
back into Atom's.

And my soul?

My Soul has been nursing a shame hangover my whole life

for having to be separate
from God.

Autumnal Eclipses: closing out karmic contracts

i: Sacred sex
An infinity loop closed circuit
energy exchange
Pinhole leaks
air escapes the balloon
keeping us pumping
Union turned
lovemaking
fucking
compulsions
No longer can I
feed the ghost
or risk compounding
karma, a juggernaut
to incarnate into

ii: Communion
Two baby gopher snakes
lay across the path
ten days apart. Parent-
theses within
the fifteen-day sentence
closing the chapter of the dance
of the seven veils written
in the Akasha book-
ending eclipses
The serpents did not slither
away when this Nāginī
reached for them charmed
Calibration in the palm of my hand
amplified and released
My temple
my mother
my lover
Nature
saves me
every time

iii: Compartmentalization
You level up
and put me in
a smaller box
to tap in
whenever you need
a hit of source
I did this
Chose it consciously
I wanted to study it
get inside
the mechanism
lust and fear
The house of sex
and death. Five scales
weighing and balancing
power and intimacy

iv: The pitch
I know you have to answer
to your board members
and I want to get my flowers
to the market
but when all is said
and done
do we really want
this to end up
just another
plastic baby Jesus?
The beginning
is where I am keeping
us filed

Signed: _____
Dated: __/__/20__

The Salesman

My husband comes home
from a hard day's work.

He drops his briefcase
on the floor and hangs
up his sickle and cloak.

I greet him with his slippers
and scotch on the rocks.

His mood is sombre
through dinner.
He barely touches his food.

We retire
to the den
and watch
the nightly news.
He's the star
of that reality show.

His 60 minutes
of knightly fame
does not lift his mood.

In bed
he gives me
the cold shoulder
"You seem distant honey,"
I ask. "Is everything okay?"
He takes a deep sigh and grumbles,
"They've found a cure for cancer."

I place my soft hand
on his shoulder bone
"Don't worry my love," I say
"There will be plenty of other contracts to fill.
You'll still be able to meet your quota."

He turns to me
and cups my tiny face
in his macilent hands.

"You're right, my darling"
He looks into me
with his blackest
of pool eyes
and presses
his icy lips
that I love
to mine
and kisses me
goodnight.

HUNTRESS

The Last Soliloquy

Karmic threads weave together in the tapestry of existence where entangled intersections become destine-nation points on the map of in-car-nations. Indeed! What dreams may come when this helical spring has sprung. Re-lease. New life bore from ashes and loam.

Unknown Void

i gave myself vertigo
scrolling yesterday, searching
for the missing tweet
the meaningful meme
to fill the emptiness
the unknown void

my offline brain
flips through the Rolodex
of inconsequential memories—

the greasy French fries
in Zihuatanejo
that gave us all the shits—

the heads turning
at the Beverly Hills hotel
me feeling both important and
not enough
at the same time—

the smell of chlorine
at the hotel pool
during Bubbie's
Bridge Tournaments—

my sister and i
swimming alone
until our lips turned blue—

the red velvet lining
of the metal heart-shaped
jewelry box
snapping shut
with a muffled clang—

the board game
at the cabin
pieces like mini wrenches
linking red and black pegs

they say when you die
your life flashes
before your eyes

mine's on slowmo
taking its sweet time
collecting all my selves
before passing through into another dimension

the thread of life
weaves its way through a
series of breaths and
gathers up memories
of identities

the abandoned
pitch tents
setting up camp
beneath the underpass
of my neuro freeways

these are the things i will leave behind—

clenched teeth
whispered screams
shushing me at two
struggling
to get off his lap

the fifty year old surfer
i met on Bumble
who muttered to himself,
"this is gonna last me a while"
before he ghosted me

these are the things i will miss—

the soft tuft of hair
on the edge of my
newborn's ear
latched onto my breast
eyes drifting closed
and open again
in the fight against sleep

the chiming leaves
of the aspen cathedral
as wind rushes
through the forest

and the crunch of
ice crystals beneath my feet
from the last spring snow

this is where I am going—

dissimulating
into the cacophony of wild birds
in Belize at dawn

dissolving
into the intense stillness
like the low flat energy
of Joshua Tree

merging
into the electric green
strobe light flash
the last kiss of the Sun
eaten by the Sea

hide n' seek

no one teaches
you shame

it's inherent
in being separate
from god

hiding—

i thought
that was
how boys play
with little girls.

seeking—

he looked up
at my perplexed little face
i didn't see shame
in his eyes

finding—

did he find what he
was looking for in there
in my panties—
did he find
God?

someone told me
it was bad
that meant
i was bad too

why else
was i made
to be separate
from god?

quiet

in my childhood room
the darkness
is an empty
silence

but for the blood
rushing in my ear
whoosh swoosh
whoosh swoosh
pressed
to the cold pillow
and the television
seeping
through the crack
at the bottom
of door

i am crushed

between
the solitude
of existence
and the evening news

the emptiness
is a compression
chamber
whoosh swoosh
whoosh swoosh
in my mother's womb
waiting
to contract
through the opening
at the bottom

i am becoming

absorbing placental
nicotine
pork rinds
and *Tab*

the silence
is single celled
and primal
whoosh swoosh
whoosh swoosh
i flounder
in the bottom
of the raging sea

The call is coming from inside the house.

I am an accomplice
to a murder
not in action but in knowledge
of the crime. Committed.
A recurring nightmare.
Victim blaming
but I am both
casualty and perpetrator.

The dream becomes a deliberate-
ration race walking to waking.
Which one of us will confess
before the alarm sounds.

The domesticated woman,
a blank canvas
for the projections
of men's repressions,
sidles up to power
instead of reclaiming her
Black Moon Lilith
for fear of being burned.

Disempowering women
allows business men's busi-
ness
overlooked
looked over
bypass
freepass
passengers
in plane sight MAGA-
zines left on
read on coffee tables
Consume.
Consume
Con-
    sue-
        me

Until you start to rearrange
the furniture and the things
that once were okay at
www.aretheseyourbodies@thepriceofdoingbusiness.com
take on new meaning with perspective.

What if healing were
as simple as a reinterpretation of
the past. Releasing all timelines
of anticipations.

I'm not available
to come to the phone
right now.

You see, I am doing
very important business
right now.

I'm not sure if
you've noticed but
it's spider season
and the baby spiders
are casting their filaments
into the wind and taking flight
right now.

I would love to share this
right now with you for likes but
you'll just have to take
my word for it
as these tiny miracles
are nearly impossible
to capture and feed
to the algorithm.

me vs me

the mean people
(the enemies)
in my head
take on
many forms
family, friends, me
and i'm tired
of fighting them
but when it's
me vs me
i surrender
so i'd rather the
enemy of the state
wear their face
so there
is enough space
between us
to fight back
and not to believe
their lies

Perfectionism

The problem
with wanting
to always be
in control
is that your
rigid world
becomes smaller
and smaller
only to find out
when life breaks you,
and it will break you,
your armor
shatters
into one million
tiny shards
of mirror

i didn't write a poem today

i didn't see the sunrise
but watched it drop from the sky
i didn't write a poem
about it
i don't want my opinions
added to the Great
Pacific garbage patch

i don't want to talk about
the beauty of things
or how horrible the world is
right now
or how i cry so easily over
nothing and everything all at once

my heaving sadness wanders
door to door looking for a home
it calls during dinner
and says
"we've been trying to reach you about your car's extended warranty"

all the birds are outraged
kerfuffled feathers
tweeting all hours
day and night
day and night
things like
"belief in apocalypse is a coping mechanism"

i dreamt about the fifth dimension
last night
it defied logic
i tried to access the formula
and pull it
into my waking hours
is that a coping mechanism too

i'm trying to move forward
i want to tie a string
to a thumbtack
in the future
so i know where to go
but life tells me
to hold still
it is not time
for answers to questions
formed
on unsteady
foundation

i went on a trip
looking for clarity
there is a minimum baggage
requirement
as we head into a
new consciousness
i was forced to purge grief
my brains spilled
out of my tear ducts
nerve strands fell
in a pile
on the linoleum

i asked to speak to the manager
 "i don't like this" i complained

"what are you going
to do about it," laughed
the fun guy, "write a bad Yelp review?"

"let's let
axons be bygones"
over came the inner calm
as they lifted me off the plane
and we head towards
ground zero

Sutra of Karma

trying to make sense
in a place of non-senses
words grasp at meaning
logic's medium for survival

Nothingness

is not a destination
outside of existence
but a dissolving into all of existence
boundless and empty

free

from the conditioning and construct
of ego and identity

i am unchained
but tied
to this body
by breath

the thread of life

Attaining Enlightenment in the Wild Wild West

impermanence
of creation

the contours
delineating

the egg
or duality

which came first

contradiction?
the infinite?

intense stillness

it is missed
at emptiness

grasping the unattainable

to describe
words do not exist

forever

unknown

destination

- I have arrived
- Bucket list complete
- Stake the claim
- Check the box

√ Enlightenment attained
4/26/2018

you will be met

if you could fold a
piece of paper
103 times

its thickness
would be larger
than the observable
universe

i turn inward
countless times
and fold into
the unobservable
space

i pull a frayed sutra
karmic constructs
woven through
this tapestry
existence

unwinding
unfolding
opening
into the
light

CRONE

Release

The gravity that binds us together with time, will also break us apart in order to return to Earth what has been borrowed, and Ether fills the spaces between to remind us whence we came.

Darn

All of my favorite socks
have holes in them.
I resist the urge to search
for an exact replacement.

My kin would
darn them
but there are only
so many holes you can repair
before it feels like walking on scars.

Whenever my sister
had something special
like a favorite magic marker
she didn't use it
but locked it away
so it wouldn't fade.

There, tucked away
safely, it dried up
never having a chance
to live up
to its potential.

A friend of hers would buy two
of anything he cherished.
One to use and
one to keep new.

My daughter has a playlist
of favorite songs
that she rarely listens to
because they're "too special"
and she doesn't want
to get tired of them.

When she was a baby
learning to walk
she pulled a cool iron down
from a low shelf onto her head.

The pointy tip made a tiny triangle
dent in her forehead.
She was fine. She didn't cry.
It didn't even bleed.

I tortured myself thinking
"I should have been closer.
Why didn't I put the iron away
or at least wind up the cord.
She's not perfect anymore
and it's my fault."

All the while she's
standing there in front of me
with a tiny hole in her head
and a perplexed look
on her little face
experiencing a new sensation.
Being alive.

I'm afraid of getting old.
But I'd like to believe
that this worn-down feeling
means that I've lived well
and have loved without fear.

De-struction

Best leave well
enough alone
said no anxious
person ever.

My first child
was born face up.
When I left
the hospital
I popped the sutures
of my labial tear
craning my neck
twisting and contorting
to check on the progress
of healing.

When she was six
waiting
for me on the
distressed
leather armchair
outside
the James Perse dressing
room
her curious fingers-

-discovered
a tiny hole.

-punctured
the worn leather.

-explored
the fluffy stuff.

-peeled
the layers of raw hide.

-exposed
what was inside.

The store manager
made us pay
for the damage.
I was upset with her
even though I understood
the urge.

At her age
I would have done
the same thing.
I still do it now.

If I see a loose thread
I am
going to pull it
and secretly hope
the universe unravels.

I've worn worry
stones down to sand
but you can't do that
with people.
It's best to leave them
where they are.

Grief

My daughters and I
found a dead dolphin
washed up on the shore
of a private beach

Its rubbery skin was intact
burnt red and blackened purple
like it had been brined
and cooked in the sun
for days, maybe weeks

The swarms of flies
did not penetrate
the casing of its bloated body
but made their way in
through its orifices

I imagined if I had sons
they would poke at it with sticks,
the way boys do when they don't
understand something,
hoping to puncture the skin
and see what was festering inside

It comes in waves
the tide
tears the flesh
from the bone
and carries it out to sea

In 1970 a dead
sperm whale
washed ashore
in Portland, Oregon

Not knowing how
to remove eight tons
of decaying flesh
the putrescine marine layer
wafted inland

They didn't want
to bury it, burn it
cut into smaller pieces
the engineer in charge
decided to decimate the carcass
with twenty cases of dynamite
the way men do when they don't
want to deal with shit

The sea decides when
to cleanse her shores
left on the ocean floor
the detritivores maintain
the ecology of the soul

Primal Urges

The wild woman
that resides in my genes
remembers anointing your
cutaneous wounds
for protection, meat
and a child.

Do not call me
from the wounded place.
She will no longer
rise to meet you
and lick your scars
to soothe
my own.

You may call me
whole.
We'll meet again
in the boundless place.

letting go

i am a fly-fishing hook ballerina
my marabou tutu twirls,
on a tightrope thread
that thins as she spins
away from the cliff
drawn into the vacuum
anchored in darkness
my recurring nightmare
reels
reels
reels
to get back
on solid ground

my daughter's umbilical cord
took too long to fall off
even after it was twice cauterized
the doctor said it's a sign
of a healthy cord
they usually begin to deteriorate
in the womb

when she was a baby
if the sun went down
during a late afternoon nap
she would wake
inconsolable
from deep sleep
pre-language
no words to soothe
no words to explain

i cradled her
tiny heaving body
patting her delicate back
chanting
it's okay
it's okay
it's okay

if i paused this mantra
to say, "did you have a bad dream"
the vacuum would suck her back
into the darkness

i'd rock her for hours
until she remembered
she was safe in my arms

the unseen cord
that ties us to this life
and connects us to each other
cannot be broken
but thins when stretched
across time

at a temple in Varanasi
i touched the bindu
of Sri Yantra
all of my cells rotated
in concentric circles
like gears in Vishnu's clock
a helical ladder
the infinite umbilical cord
connecting life
to a black hole
nothingness
opposite ends of the same
wormhole
stretched between
consciousness and nonexistence

in the in-between
the ether thins
i twirl and dance
drawn to nothingness

density cannot sustain
in this atom sphere
there is
no i
no other
no holding on

the cord thins
the tightrope becomes a frayed
thread and unravels

the filaments
of our attachment
have become threadbare,
my Love,

to free us
from suffering
i have to let go

Night Mer

I astral traveled
to the confluence
of Lethe and Styx.

My brother-in-law
Hypnos welcomed me
with a bouquet of poppies.

He showed me
a whirlpool of collective
consciousness churning
detritus of the human psyche

to be picked over
and sorted later by
my husband and him.

Two brothers
trading baseball cards.

redwood

the fallen redwood
never dies
it lives in everything
it has ever touched
in the mist
that kissed
its uppermost branches

its ancient essence
gathered and condensed
in droplets
reigning reining raining
down
the forest canopy
lapped up by the drunken bumblebee
and turned to honey

it is carried on the wind
that has circled the globe
for thousands of years past
and thousands more to come

it lives in the soil
its crawling roots
cloning fairy circle colonies
nourished by their progenitors' decay

it lives in the fire's
ash-filtered light
enveloping the ether
like a chiffon curtain
woven with gold and amber silk

and buried deep beneath
the soot and loam
thousands of tiny seeds
live nestled inside
its baby cones
waiting to reach
for the sun

Welcoming the Witch

I've been writing poems
to fill this empty cup
nest woven of sticks and bark
grasses and dried flowers
lined with molted feathers and now
words. Everything is an offering
to my altar while I wait
for my next assignment.

When my children were young
I used to say, that their successes are theirs
but their failures are mine.

I don't know why I believed
that. Like there was something
noble in saving them from suffering.
Haven't those moments of despair
hatched my greatest lessons? What more
has loss come to teach me? They are
thriving. I should be celebrating. Do I dare
admit I'd like to be celebrated?

Everyone keeps asking,
"Are you going to downsize now
that both girls are at college?"
And I don't mean to be rude but,
Fuck you. I built this nest.
They wouldn't even be asking me that
if I had some Cuckoo Bird
still here to tend to. I've chosen
to recalibrate with my own energy
instead of nurturing someone else's child.

The other day I was on my way
out when I heard something hit
the window and rushed to find
a Cedar Waxwing twitching
on the cold concrete. I scooped him up
hoping to revive him in the warmth
of my hands. The vacancy crept in,
first through the eyes, his tufted crown
crestfallen, his feet curled grasping
the ethereal Yew as his spirit took flight.
I wrapped his body in a cloth napkin
and placed it inside an Amazon Prime

box on the porch 'til mourning.
A Red-Tailed Hawk watched me
from a nearby branch as I harvested
the Waxwing's yellow-tipped tail feathers.
Nothing wasted. Not even death.

The faith keepers, the shepherds
of solitude, assure me to stay
the course. The Bobcat that bounded
down the mountainside across
Mulholland in front of my car,
his golden coat glistening in the late
afternoon sun, rippling over
every muscle. It happened
so fast in slow motion.

And the next afternoon, again
on Mulholland, the Stag that lept
across the road in front of my car
then stopped on the other side of the guard-
rail to look over his shoulder at me
when I slowed and rolled down
the window to express my gratitude
for the gift of his presence.

I've been returning the calls
of the owl outside my bedroom
window. His droppings splattered beneath
my balcony when I awoke. Then
yesterday, just home from my afternoon
walk, a fresh gift of wet sloppy fur
and bones. The Great Horned Owl
perched on the oak branch above
stared down at me with his big unblinking
yellow eyes. I bowed to him and placed
his offering in a Prime box
to sort through once it is dry.

I guess you could call these encounters
coincidence, pattern recognition,
meaning-making, magical thinking,
but I believe serendipity
and coincidence is God giving
me a thumbs up. It is not lost on me,
these blessings. It feels like I'm living
in a fairytale with all of these woodland
creatures that have come to fill my cup
in celebration of the Crone.

Earthly Cravings

I'm done contemplating
the meaning of life

All of my seeking
has been to reach
a boundless state
of intense stillness
while coral reefs die

Rising temperatures
in the sea
bleach white
varietal gardens
of colorful beings
and cover them in algae

Men in power deny
so why spend time
trying to determine
what purpose existence serves

Who am I to ascribe
value or meaning
when God doesn't differentiate

Doesn't *he*
love all of *his*
creation equally?

Life is life
whether
coral or algae

Algae can be seen
as beautiful too

Sagan said we are a way
for the cosmos to know itself

God reaches out
to touch the hand of man

I can't help think
God is a narcissist

A blue whale's heart
slows, two beats
per minute
when it dives deep
into the sea

The red light of Betelgeuse
ebbs and flows
yet Orion still wields
his mighty club

The Earth pulsates
every twenty-six seconds

She is alive
therefore
I
am

When I am permitted
to leave the flesh
will I long for Life
like my earthly craving
to be one
with Everything

If a tree screams in the forest and no one hears, did it fall?

On a solo walk in the wilderness,
seeking a cypher, a symbol, an omen,
a metaphor, a prophesy, any kind of sign
from the planetary shift I have been under
the influence of for the past six years,
I came across an entangled tree
in a dried-out riverbed.

Her roots had been spread open at the base
and a vaginal tree hollow spilled forth
a mass of fleshy matter.

Her branches were pinned to her sides
by an invasive vine that had climbed up
her elongated stump and strangled her
just below a massive gall.

It looked as if the brambly monster,
mounted behind her, was pulling her
head back by the hair while she screamed.

She screamed for life.

Not hers.

Not the unformed mass she was forced
to bear and birth into a dried-out riverbed.

She screamed for her dying mother
and the men that only see the feminine form
as vessels for their seed.

She screams
because as she is the bringer of life;
she is also the doula of death
fully aware that consciousness
need not form.

Photograph by Taryn Weitzman

About the author

Nicole Cannon is a writer, actor and producer based in Los Angeles. She wrote and produced her third screenplay, a psychological thriller, *Transference*, available on Amazon.

Her poetry has been featured in publications such as *Elephant Journal, Words & Whispers* Issue 12, *Side Eye on the Apocalypse Anthology, ONTHEBUS* 23 & 25, and *Writers Speak* #2 & #4. *A Woman in Pieces* is Nicole's first full-length collection of poems.